Ways to....

MOVE *it!*

Henry Pluckrose

Photography by Chris Fairclough

FRANKLIN WATTS

London • New York • Sydney • Toronto

Have you ever wondered how things move?

If you let go of an object, it drops to the ground. Our planet earth pulls everything towards it. This pull is called gravity.

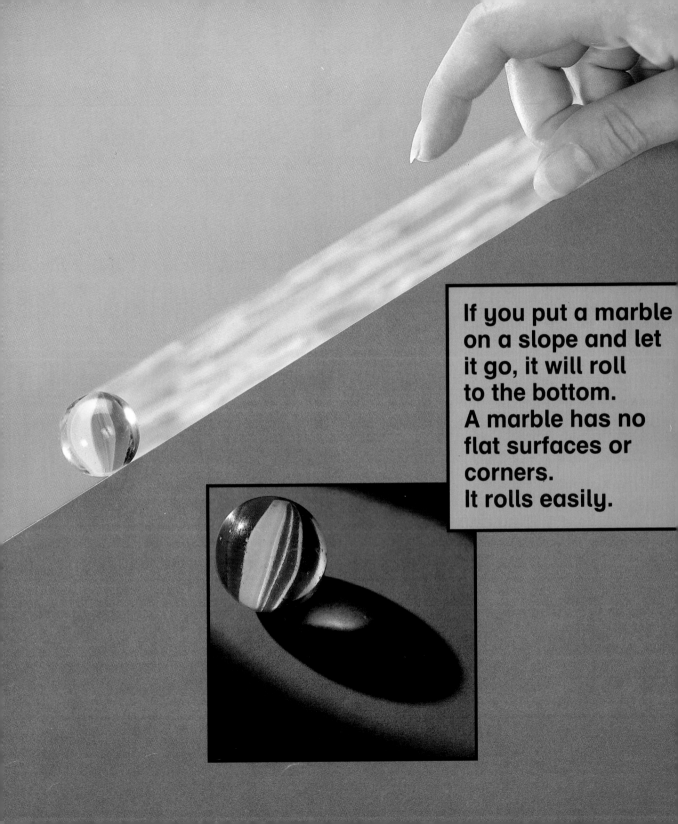

If you put a marble
on a slope and let
it go, it will roll
to the bottom.
A marble has no
flat surfaces or
corners.
It rolls easily.

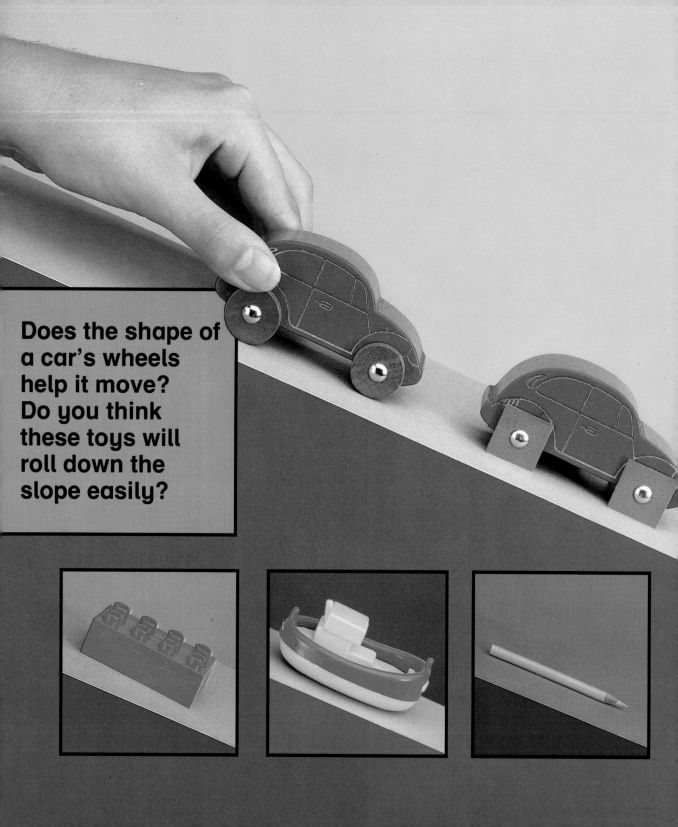

Does the shape of a car's wheels help it move? Do you think these toys will roll down the slope easily?

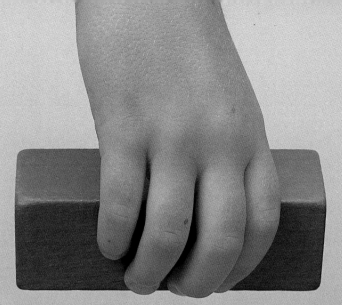

Things cannot move upwards or along a surface without some kind of power. We can push a car, lift a brick or flick a marble.

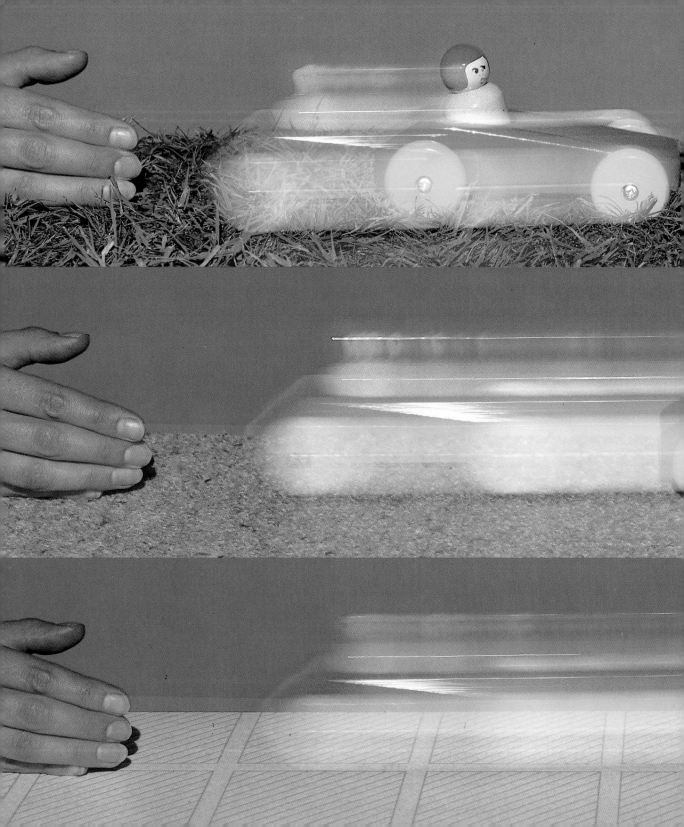

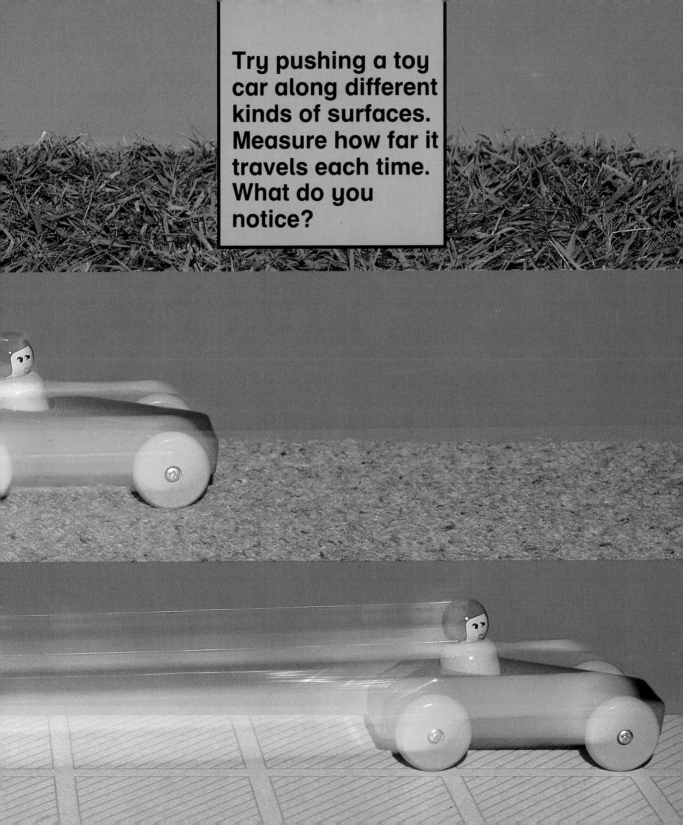

Try pushing a toy car along different kinds of surfaces. Measure how far it travels each time. What do you notice?

Think how many ways you can move your body. What gives you the power to move?

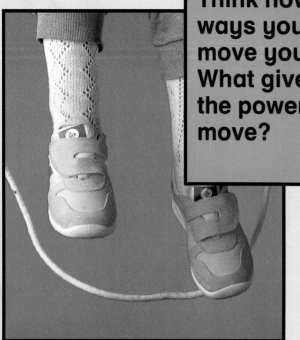
skipping

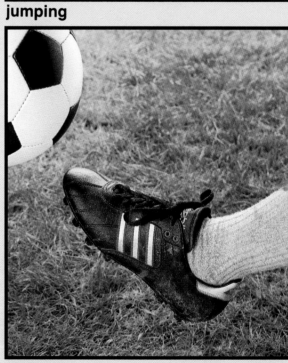
jumping

throwing

kicking

walking

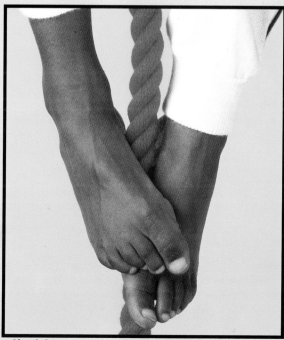

dancing

swimming

climbing

You can use these things to make you move faster.
What do they have in common?

skateboard

roller skates

bike

scooter

You can use machines like these to make work easier. Can you think of any others?

screwdriver

wheelbarrow

pulley

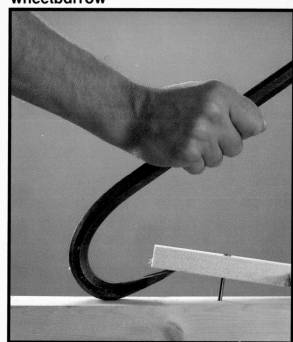

crow bar

Water can move things. The force of running water turns both these waterwheels.

Streams and rivers run downwards to the sea. Things that float on the surface move along the rushing water.

Wind provides power to move things. Moving air catches in the sails of windmills and makes them turn.

Wind fills the sails of yachts and pushes them across water.

Some things have a motor inside. Electric power makes them move. The power comes from batteries or the electric mains.

Big machines move by burning fuel to provide power. Coal and oil are important fuels.

Cars use petrol (made from oil).

Trucks use diesel fuel (made from oil).

Jets use kerosene (made from oil).

Steam engines use coal.

What sort of power makes these things move?

car

see-saw

ice skates

jack-in-a-box

watch

bath toy

crane

football

Things to do

Make a windmill

You will need:

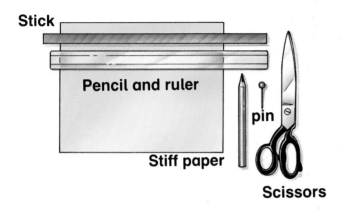

Stick

Pencil and ruler

Stiff paper

pin

Scissors

2. Draw lines from corner to corner.

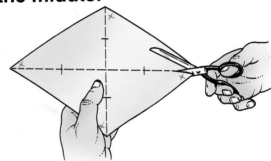

3. Cut along the lines halfway from the corners to the middle.

1. Cut a square of stiff paper.

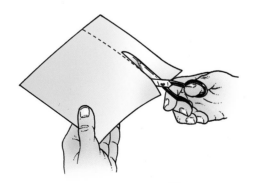

4. Fold the starred corners into the middle and pin them to a stick with a push pin.

Making a paper dart

Make a paper dart by folding a piece of paper like this:

1. Fold it in half lengthways to find the centre and then open it out again.

2. Fold the two top corners inwards to the centre.

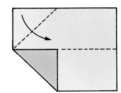

3. Turn the paper over. Fold the two long sides to the centre.

4. Open out the sides to make a dart like this.

Fly your dart in the open air. To improve its flight, you may need to alter the nose fold, making it either bigger or smaller.

Launch your dart first into the wind and then with the wind to see a difference in the way it flies.

Words about moving

charge	glide	slip
clamber	hop	slither
climb	hurry	speed
crawl	jump	spin
creep	leap	step
dance	march	stride
dawdle	plod	swim
dive	pull	swing
drop	push	swoop
fall	roll	tremble
flick	run	trot
flit	rush	tug
float	shake	turn
flow	shiver	twirl
flutter	skate	twist
fly	skip	walk
gallop	slide	zoom